Late August

poems

Barbara Brackney

Pleasure Boat Studio: A Literary Press
New York

Late August

No. 12 in the Pleasure Boat Studio Chapbook Series

Poems by Barbara Brackney © 2009

ISBN 978-1-929355-58-7

A portion (20%) of the proceeds from the sale of this book will be donated to the Susan B. Komen Breast Cancer Foundation. A further portion (10%) will be donated to Alcoholics Anonymous.

From pgmsimone, her life companion of lo some three decades as her surrogate voice, comes the credit: 'Jason, you have been immensly helpful, both as editor and as agent, to the publication of the following words, which I hope—at least in some instance, were as helpful for someone to read as they were for me to write. God bless the existence of human interconnection, yours, mine, and that of all us wonderfully, if at times invisibly, interconnected human beings.'

Pleasure Boat Studio is a proud subscriber to the Green Press Initiative. This program encourages the use of 100% post-consumer recycled paper with environmentally friendly inks for all printing projects in an effort to reduce the book industry's economic and social impact. With the cooperation of our printing company, we are pleased to offer this book as a Green Press book.

Pleasure Boat Studio books are available through the following:
SPD (Small Press Distribution) Tel. 800-869-7553, Fax 510-524-0852
Partners/West Tel. 425-227-8486, Fax 425-204-2448
Baker & Taylor 800-775-1100, Fax 800-775-7480
Ingram Tel 615-793-5000, Fax 615-287-5429
Amazon.com and bn.com

and through
PLEASURE BOAT STUDIO: A LITERARY PRESS
www.pleasureboatstudio.com
201 West 89th Street
New York, NY 10024

Contact Jack Estes
Fax; 888-810-5308
Email: pleasboat@nyc.rr.com

Table of Contents

For George Simone, my true love of thirty years

WHERE THINGS STAND

My nipple turned inward, back into my self.

The biopsy said Lobular Breast Cancer.

Metastatic.

*

Then: the unpronounceable:

      adriamyacinzometaaratomase.
      inhibitorgemzataxateretamoxifenxeloda.

Then: navelbine.
      (Chemo)

*

Then: nothing.

Except
      1) oxycontin
      2) morphine
      3) waiting for my liver to fail

*

Life expectancy: nine months
      (1, 2, 3, 4, 5, 6, 7, 8, 9)
      starting a month ago.

six of the months
(1, 2, 3, 4, 5, 6)
are expected to be good.

*

Everyone says I look radiant.

Everyone says I have high color.

I must be Autumn.

I'll smell good burning.

THREE MONTHS AGO

I said, "He's saying that
I have a year left to live,"

and she said, "You've always
been such a pessimist.

"Look how long you've lived so far,
you're going to live a long time yet."

I wanted to be told
that I would be missed.

I wanted to be told
that I would be remembered.

She said, "Look at you:
You're the same

as you've always been.
At the rate you're going,

you'll probably outlive me."
She laughed softly,

and we'll never speak
again.

Beware of Beauty

Take care when you choose
from the cage which to free
because they may turn back
to torment you.

BILOXI

Here's mom and me fishing.

Look again.

We're not smiling.

See the newspaper to wrap the fish?

It's empty.

Catfish need to be hooked, beheaded,

gutted, scaled, leached of poisons

in salt water

for a long hour,

then filleted.

It's hard to wait.

Our mouths water.

Our tempers are short.

If we catch no fish,

we'll eat only eggs,

the ones parceled out to the poor.

Some have blood spots.

Some have curled up chicks.

Sex from Three to Twenty: As Yet Unrevised

1.

Sex began with *Ferdinand, the Friendly Bull.*
At night in my crib, I straddled a pillow,
moving up and down, while imagining
the bull's tongue and how it might feel—
rough and soft and warm—
moving up on my exposed, greedy skin.

2.

Until nine or ten, sex was mean and sexless—
I was the queen in charge of who was strapped
to the punish machine which was like a circling
waterwheel, but with paddles that slapped pink butts
until they were red and swollen.
I could pee on the person if I wanted.

3.

When my friend Helen spent the night,
we decided to rub each other's
belly in slow, soothing circles;
when she did me, her hand was so warm
that I couldn't help pulling her wrist lower so the warmth
went right through my cotton crotch.
I never wanted my turn to be over.

4.

In the years when clothes had to stay mostly on,
my lover was the seam in my jeans:
I'd get a boy—just about any of them would do—
on top and I'd grab him with my legs
so the vertical lump of the seam would slide sideways
bumping over and over the secret hot bump of me.

Later, I'd insist that we sit facing each other
so that I could grind around and around
instead of the in and out guys always chose.
I'd laugh as I counted how many times
I could come at the end of
"Hey, Jude" with John singing over the rest.

TIME FOR SOME HELP

We're down to the poverty eggs,

so Mom knows she'd better get married.

She found the Sergeant last night

and now she's giving him the treatment.

That's why she left me at this rooming house.

I make bacon grease and sugar sandwiches

for breakfast and lunch.

A woman makes dinner.

I don't have to talk to anybody.

There's a huge stack of comics to read.

I know she'll hook the guy.

I know things will be better.

THE WONDER

One day I went with mom
to hard clean the houses.

The house was ten times bigger
than the biggest I'd ever seen.

I explored the rooms and found
a bracelet of gold roses.

One rose popped up when I pressed it,
showing a weeny watch.

Something inside me broke—
my balance broke.

There was another world
I had to get to.

A Stupid Book

The *Van-something Guide to a Happy Marriage*
was hidden on the high shelf of the hall closet.

I got it down on the floor,
held the drawing to face the wall,

sat up without moving the book.
I scootched around to understand the angle.

Then I got a mirror
and pulled my jeans down.

That thing with the hairy fringe and dark hole
didn't look a bit like me or my friends.

Lost

Who dims the light?

Who brings the black?

Who starts the silence?

I am lost.

I am here.

Not hearing makes silence.

Not seeing makes black.

May I leave this black?

I want to move

above this.

I want to be with you.

THE UNSPOKEN

Mothers speak of sex in words
of safety, caution, babies.

Maybe they're confused themselves,
revolted by their sexual baby,

angry, cheated by a clumsy husband,
or ashamed of night times' wildness.

Still, I found the instinct:
legs spread wide, hips high,

eyes wide.

My Every Thought

A complete sentence
Is comforting.

it solves the problem.

A History of Altered States

After smoking my first joint,
I ate a jar of peanut butter
a jar of cold spaghetti sauce,
and then barfed on the carpet.

*

I breathed in and out
from the balloons of nitrous,
and came to with a long green
drool of snot for everyone to see.

*

My work friends and I refreshed ourselves
several times daily with coke,
certain that we were better for it—
so much more empathy and energy.

*

When I ran out of Dexamyl,
I took the other pills: the ones
with a touch of strychnine
that did the job almost as well.

*

When the daily Absolut grew to just under
a fifth, I took to driving around around town
with a .38 tucked under the front seat
just in case this was the solution.

AMONG THE LIVING

looking at your face
I forget my own face

my bed socks begin
to warm my winter feet

your understanding is a hand
lifting me from the floor

I'm leaving the party
too soon

My Brother's Plan, Imagined
For JRP

Stop Whining.

Drive to K-mart. Buy a long-billed baseball cap.
trash bags (black, not transparent), a bungy cord,
and plastic tubing (half inch diameter, four feet).

Then a toy store. Rent helium in a canister to blow
up balloons. It's a birthday party for my son (lie).

At the liquor store, a fifth and ice.

At Jeff's or George's. Find their hypertension pills.
Steal five.

Choose the day.
Tell folks I'll be out of town.

Toss all my ID because (ha)
I have no identity.

Book a room in another name.
Back my car in to hide the license plates.

Spread my stash and a pillow on the table.
Drag up a chair—sit down.

Swig the liquor a couple times. More.
As needed.

Swallow the pills.

Attach the tubing to the gas tank.

Stuff some cash in an envelope.
Write: To Maid.

Go piss. Avoid mirrors.
Have a seat.
Scoop out ice with my cap about halfway.
Pop it on. Drink more. Drink more,
Drink more.

Ease the black bag over my head.
The cap's bill keeps the plastic from
my face. Snake the tubing up over my ear.

Sneak some booze under the bag.
Drink again.

Clip the cord and hold it away

Breathe easy.

Breathe easy.

AFTERWARDS

You are bones.
Charred shards.

I spoon a spoonful
and drink them,

with water,
taste in tact.

There's a wound
that won't heal.

You are in me.
And in the ash

of my bones
will be you.

THE DIAGONAL

They had a graph
with two lines:
the x axis—tumor size;
the y-axis—time.

Each new node
burns brightly:
buckshot in her vertebrae;
constellations in her liver

They plotted the points
for a climbing diagonal.
The line over time
reaches one destination

it's a dull drama,
this rising line
to which one more
point is added.

Late August

In late August, the cicadas' siren saws.
High summer's flowers are finished.

Yet the gladioli tall stems reveal
hot orange centers one by one.

The daylilies still open florid red flowers
for a day; another will bloom tomorrow.

The sedum waits for its show,
still tightly green with pink secrets.

The violet foxgloves under the snow crab
return, a late summer surprise.

Trees are tipped with fire colors
before cold nakedness returns.

I flare farther, staggering, stunned.

AFTERWORD

Barbara came to poetry late, but she came to it with a ferocity and determination that made up for lost time. I met her a student in a class I was teaching for the Gotham Writers' Workshop, and she immediately stood out. She had no time for small talk, no time for digressions or evasions. She wanted to discuss serious prosodic concerns, all the time, and with great intensity. It was thrilling to have a student's attention so completely.

I soon found out that the intensity of Barbara's study stemmed from the fact that she knew she was dying. She wanted to leave something of herself in the world, and she wanted to leave it in poems. I have to admit that I was a bit skeptical of the idea at the time. It worried me deeply that she would most likely not be able to reach the level of achievement she wanted in the short time she had. And yet I recognized in her a calling and a dedication that was impossible to ignore. She took a few more classes, and then we began to work intensively over the summer of 2007 on the manuscript that became the chapbook you are now holding.

I never met Barbara face to face. The classes were online, and our correspondence was by e-mail. She lived in Michigan and I lived in New York. Her voice for me is what's captured in these poems. Barbara's poems are at once precise and plain spoken. She nurtured a sense of urgency and directness in her work, paring down her stories to the salient detail that might illustrate the whole. I love how honest and revealing her poems are, how she achieved her goal of remaining in these pages. In one of Barbara's last letters to me, anticipating the gathering of her Care Group she wrote, "I suppose there is supposed to be a sad tinge to this time but I am high as a kite on the love I have for all of them and it feels like a celebration." That's what I hope this chapbook will feel like. A celebration.

-Jason Schneiderman
Brooklyn, 2009

ACKNOWLEDGMENTS

Grateful acknowledgments are made to the following journals where these poems first appeared (sometimes in other forms and versions).

Arch. and Quiver: "The Unspoken"

Children, Churches & Daddies: "Time for Some Help"

Cloven Spheres: "My Brother's Plan"

Darkling Magazine: "The Diagonal," "Guises"

Sunken Lines: "The Wonder," "Biloxi"

Our Chapbook Series

No. 1: *The Handful of Seeds: Three and a Half Essays* * Andrew Schelling * $7 * nonfiction

No. 2: *Original Sin* * Michael Daley * $8 * poetry

No. 3: *Too Small to Hold You* * Kate Reavey * $8 * poetry

No. 4: *The Light on Our Faces: A Therapy Dialogue* * Lee Miriam Whitman-Raymond * $8 * poetry

No. 5: *Eye* * William Bridges * $8 * poetry

No. 6: *Selected New Poems of Rainer Maria Rilke* * trans. fm German by Alice Derry * $10 * poetry

No. 7: *Through High Still Air: A Season at Sourdough Mountain* * Tim McNulty * $9 * poetry, prose

No. 8: *Sight Progress* * Zhang Er, trans. fm Chinese by Rachel Levitsky * $9 * prose poems

No. 9: *The Perfect Hour* * Blas Falconer * $9 * poetry

No. 10: *Fervor* * Zaedryn Meade * $10 * poetry

No. 11: *Some Ducks* * Tim McNulty * $10 * poetry

No. 12: *Late August* * Barbara Brackney * $10 * poetry

No. 13: *The Right to Live Poetically* * Emily Haines * $10 * poetry

Barbara Brackney spent her youth living in the deep south, California and Europe. She received her doctorate in clinical psychology from the University of Michigan and resolved to make Ann Arbor her lifetime home. After graduation, she became a professor of psychology, had a clinical private practice and spent her free time traveling. In 1998, she retired quite early, eager to explore aspects of life that working precludes. One of these avenues was poetry, which opened up an exciting world of inner exploration. Barbara developed terminal cancer but this only fueled her desire to continue in her poetry quest. She died in 2007.